1&2 PETER

LECTIO DIVINA FOR YOUTH

1&2 PETER

LECTIO DIVINA FOR YOUTH

ANCIENT FAITH SERIES

Barefoot Ministries®
Kansas City, Missouri

Copyright © 2008 by Barefoot Ministries®

ISBN 978-0-8341-5025-6

Printed in the United States of America

Written by Tim Guptill
Editor: Mike Wonch
Contributing Editor: Bo Cassell
Assistant Editor: Robyn M. Boss
Assistant Editor: Stephanie McNelly
Cover Design: JR Caines
Interior Design: Sharon Page

Adapted from *Lectio Divina Bible Studies: Listening for God Through 1 & 2 Peter.*

Guptill, Tim. *Lectio Divina Bible Studies: Listening for God Through 1 & 2 Peter.* Indianapolis, IN: Wesleyan Publishing House and Beacon Hill Press of Kansas City, 2006.

Library of Congress Control Number: 2008929043

10 9 8 7 6 5 4 3 2 1

ABOUT THE
LECTIO DIVINA
BIBLE STUDIES

Lectio divina (pronounced lek-tsee-oh dih-vee-nuh) is a Latin phrase that means *sacred reading.* It is the ancient Christian practice of communicating with God through the reading and study of Scripture. Throughout history, great Christian leaders have used and adapted this ancient method of interpreting Scripture.

The idea behind *lectio divina* is to look at a Bible passage in such a way that Bible study becomes less about study and more about listening. The approach is designed to focus our attention on what God is saying to us through the Word. Through the process of *lectio divina* we not only read to understand with our minds, but we read to hear with our hearts and obey. It is a way of listening to God through His Word.

Some throughout history have said that *lectio divina* turns Bible study on its head—normally we read the Bible, but in *lectio divina, the Bible reads us.* That is probably a good way to describe it. It is God using His Word in a conversation with us to read into our lives and speak to our hearts.

In this series, we will use the traditional *lectio divina* model. We have expanded each component so that it can be used by both individuals and by groups. Each session in this study includes the following elements. (Latin words and their pronunciation are noted in parentheses.)

- **Reading** (*Lectio* "lek-tsee-oh"). We begin with a time of quieting ourselves prior to reading. Then we take a slow, careful reading of a passage of Scripture. We focus our minds on the central theme of the passage. When helpful, we read out loud or read the same passage over and over several times.

- **Meditation** (*Meditatio* "medi-tah-tsee-oh"). Next, we explore the meaning of the Bible passage. Here we dig deep to try to understand all of what God might be saying to us. We think on the passage. We explore the images, and pay attention to the emotions and feelings that the passage provides. We put ourselves in the story. We look for particular words or phrases that leap off the page as the Spirit begins to speak to us through the Word.

- **Prayer** (*Oratio* "or-ah-tsee-oh"). As we meditate on the passage, we respond to God by communicating with Him. We specifically ask God to speak to us through His Word. We begin to dialog with Him about what we have read. We express praise, thanksgiving, confession, or agreement to God. And we listen. We wait before Him in silence, allowing God the chance to speak.

- **Contemplation** (*Contemplatio* "con-tehm-plah-tsee-oh"). At this point in our conversation through the Word, we come to a place where we rest in the presence of God. Our study is now about receiving what He has said to us. Imagine two old friends who have just talked at length—and now without words, they just sit together and enjoy each other's presence. Having spent time listening to God, we know a little better how God is shaping the direction of our lives. Here there is a yielding of oneself to God's will. We resolve to act on the message of Scripture.

GROUP STUDY

This book is designed to be useful for both individual and group study. To use this in a group, you may take one of several approaches:

- **Individual Study/Group Review**. Make sure each member of the group has a copy of the book. Have them read through one section during the week. (They will work through the same passage or portions of it each day that week.) Then, when you meet together, review what thoughts, notes, and insights the members of the group experienced in their individual study. Use the group questions at the end of the section as a guide.

- **Group Lectio**. Make sure each member of the group has a copy of the book. Have them read through one section during the week in individual study. When you meet together as a group, you will study the passage together through a reading form similar to lectio divina:

○ **First, read the passage out loud several times to the group**. Group members respond by waiting in silence and letting God speak.

○ **Second, have the passage read aloud again to the group once or twice more**. Use different group members for different voices, and have them read slowly. Group members listen for a word or two that speaks to them, and share it with the group. Break into smaller groups if appropriate.

○ **Third, read the passage out loud again, and have the group pray together to ask God what He might be saying to each person, and to the group as a whole.** Go around and share what each person is learning from this process. At this point, review together the group questions at the end of the section.[1]

• **Lectio Divina Steps for Groups**. Make sure each member has a copy of the book. As a group, move through the study together, going through each of the parts: reading, mediation, prayer, and contemplation. Be sure to use the group questions at the end of the section.

The important thing about using *lectio divina* in a group is to remember that this is to be incarnational ("in the flesh")—in other words, we begin to live out the Word in our community. We carry God's Word in us, (in the flesh, or incarnate in us) and we carry that Word into our group to be lived out among them.

The *Lectio Divina Bible Studies* invite readers to slow down, read Scripture, meditate upon it, and prayerfully respond to God's Word.

---

1. Parts of the "Group Lectio" section adapted from Tony Jones, *The Sacred Way: Spiritual Practices for Everyday Life*, Grand Rapids: Zondervan, 2005, p. 54.

CONTENTS

INTRODUCTION

The apostle Paul may have been a better writer and evangelist, but the apostle Peter was an eyewitness to the glory of Christ. With Jesus from His baptism, through His ministry, at His trial, crucifixion, resurrection, and finally His ascension, Peter saw it all—up close and personal. He may not have been able to process his experiences right away, but he was there, proving to be a credible and helpful source.

After years of following Christ, spreading the Word, and making disciples, Peter had earned a hearing, and he had a few things to say to the groups of believers scattered across the provinces of Asia Minor.

The two Epistles named after Peter were likely written between A.D. 64-67, the second one being the date church tradition holds as Peter's martyrdom under Nero. It is likely that Peter wrote from Rome, calling his location "Babylon"—a common, symbolic name for Rome referring to its corruption.

The first letter is about encouragement—to persevere under persecutions, to bear the name of Christ with honor despite the trying times they were suffering. In it he encouraged first-century believers to conduct themselves with actions and attitudes that would bring credit to Christ, even from a world that wanted to hate and discredit them.

The second letter was written near the close of Peter's life and emphasized the unchanging truths of Christ in contrast to false teachings that were finding their way into the church. To affirm his authority and fight those false teachings with the confirmed truth, Peter wrote, "We did not follow cleverly invented stories when we told you about the power and coming of our Lord Jesus Christ, but we were eyewitnesses of his majesty" (2 Pet. 1:16).

Peter's closing charge to the first-century church—written with knowledge of Jesus' return and his own approaching martyrdom—rings true today. "But grow in the grace and knowledge of our Lord and Savior Jesus Christ. To him be glory both now and forever! Amen" (2 Pet. 3:18).

FAITH: TRIED, TESTED, AND TRUE
LISTENING FOR GOD THROUGH 1 PETER 1:1-12

SUMMARY

Most of us don't enjoy tests. Whether it's undergoing a medical examination, getting your driver's permit, or taking the ACT, tests can be stressful. Even so, we all experience them.

Peter, too, had his share of tests. He experienced firsthand his faith being tested to the limit. But Peter also knew the amazing feeling of passing a test and receiving the reward for his effort and endurance.

Some days can seem like a series of tests. We may feel as though we are only one decision away from passing or failing. Yet we turn in our papers to God—all of the right and all of the wrong—and we commit it all to Him.

Peter learned that God's tests have eternal rewards. Your faith, like Peter's, which is worth more than gold to God, can grow stronger through every test and trial.

PREPARATION ☦ FOCUS YOUR THOUGHTS

Think of a time when you failed a test. How did you feel?

Now, remember a time when you prepared for a test and passed it. How did you feel?

What are some rewards to passing life's daily tests?

READING ☦ HEAR THE WORD

Holiness. Suffering. Mercy. Testing. Peter's first letter is one of hope and encouragement. Hope, because we know what Christ has done for us. Encouragement, because we're never alone in any trial.

In this life, it's not a question of *if* trials will come but *when* they will come. When we realize that trials are inevitable, we can prepare spiritually for anything that may come our way. This is the message of 1 Peter.

It's been said that you don't know the strength of your anchor until it has weathered the storm. Think about a time when you saw a news report of an approaching storm and how people were preparing for the severe weather.

As you read these opening verses of 1 Peter, try to imagine Peter's environment and the political/religious climate. It's a few decades after Christ's resurrection. Nero is reigning over most of the known world. It's just after the great fire in Rome, and Christian persecution is widespread. Feel the sense of urgency. Sense Peter's passion. He has a message that must get out. "Don't give up. Live a life of holiness. Be filled with joy!"

Read the first 12 verses of this book slowly and purposefully. They were relevant then. They are relevant now.

MEDITATION ✝ ENGAGE THE WORD

Meditate on 1 Peter 1:1-2

Peter the apostle. This is obviously a new and improved Peter, one who had matured since his earlier days with the Master. *Apostle* means one sent on a mission. What do you think Peter's mission was?

Have you ever felt that God was giving you a mission? Did you obey? What type of mission did God call you to go on?

Spend a few moments quietly asking God if there is a mission or purpose that He may be asking you to fulfill. Write down any thoughts or key words that come to your mind. At the same time, pray for another person in your life that is getting ready to embark on their own personal mission.

Read the quote by Billy Sunday on page 16. We often look to people with the most talent to provide us with examples. Yet,

God is looking for those who know their purpose and who will follow it at any cost. Do you know your purpose? What steps could you take in the next few days to follow through with the purpose God has for your life?

> *More men fail through lack of purpose than lack of talent.*
> —Billy Sunday

Think of how many times a day you obey someone. (Parents, teachers, coaches, and so on.) Do you find it easy to obey God? Why do you think obedience is so important to Him? Are there things in your life right now that are keeping you from doing what you know He would want you to do?

Read the quote by John Wesley. Stop at the end of each sentence and allow time for reflection. To recognize the real meaning of this quote, take out the word *you* and insert your name.

> *God loves you; therefore love and obey Him. Christ died for you; therefore die to sin. Christ is risen; therefore rise in the image of God. Christ liveth ever more; therefore live to God till you live with Him in glory. So we preached; and so you believed! God grant we may never turn therefrom to the right hand or to the left.*
> —John Wesley

Meditate on 1 Peter 1:3-9

If grace is getting what we don't deserve—forgiveness—then mercy is not getting what we do deserve—punishment. When Peter mentions mercy in verse 3, he is speaking from experience. As he thinks about the new life he has been given in Christ and all of his second chances, he reminds us that without mercy we would not have hope.

Read Ephesians 2:4, and take time to reflect on how God wants to speak words of mercy and grace to you today. In your own words, write what God's mercy means to you. In what ways can you see His mercy at work in your life?

Peter's encouragement builds as he says in verse 4 that a believer's inheritance will never perish, spoil, or fade. Another contemporary version of the text puts it this way: "For God has reserved a priceless inheritance for his children. It is kept in heaven for you, pure and undefiled, beyond the reach of change and decay" (NLT). In the face of severe persecution and trials, how must the assurance of an indestructible, incorruptible, unshakable faith have boosted the readers' hope? How does it increase the depth of your own hope?

If your faith is "of greater worth than gold" as Peter says, how does that change the way you think of your salvation? Look up or discuss other uses of the word *gold* as you think about the value of your faith.

Meditate on 1 Peter 1:10-12

This section of the Scripture is like morning fog that fades as the afternoon sunshine comes closer. It was hard for the prophets to understand how or when salvation would come to earth. But now, we can see clearly what the Spirit has revealed to us—Christ has come! How does knowing Christ has come and is alive today affect your hope and level of encouragement each day?

The last part of verse 12 is another reminder of how privileged we are. Salvation, faith, and hope are all privileges of grace, respected even by angels. Of all created by the Creator, humans can be redeemed, forgiven, and adopted into God's family. And angels look on. Think for a moment of your most valuable possession. What makes it valuable? Think of your faith in similar terms. What makes it valuable to you and to God?

PRAYER ⚜ ASK AND LISTEN

Seek the face of God. Ask, "Lord, what are You saying to us today?"

Rejoicing through real-life trials is Peter's challenge and encouragement to us. Take as much time as you need to pray the following prayer: "Lord, show me how I can trust You always and in all ways. Teach me to rejoice in every situation. Remind me again of the eternal value of my faith."

CONTEMPLATION ⚜ REFLECT AND YIELD

Read the quote from Charles Spurgeon. How does it make you feel?

> *Faith untried may be true faith, but it is sure to be little faith, and it is likely to remain dwarfish so long as it is without trials. Faith never prospers so well as when all things are against her.* —Charles Spurgeon

GROUP STUDY

- What is your definition of obedience?

- Look back in this chapter where it says, "If grace is getting what we don't deserve—forgiveness—then mercy is not getting what we do deserve—punishment." Have you ever thought about that before? How does this make you feel?

- How would you describe God's mercy in your own words?

- How can you trust God more in every situation?

- If you were to face persecution tomorrow—a trial or some kind of spiritual battle—how would you handle it?

- Do you consider your faith a "greater worth than gold"? If so, why?

- Write down the things that test your faith most. What will you do this week to pass these tests and show evidence of God's mercy at work in your life?

TIME TO GROW UP
LISTENING FOR GOD THROUGH
I PETER 1:13—2:3

SUMMARY

We are born to grow. Healthy things grow. We see many examples in God's creation that growth is natural and expected. There are also many biblical metaphors of growth that remind us of our responsibility. Ephesians 4:14-15 reads, "Then we will no longer be infants . . . we will . . . grow up into him who is the Head."

Knowing that we need to grow spiritually is not enough. Spiritual growth requires a call to action. It is the work of the Holy Spirit, but it is not automatic.

When you want something to grow straight, you place stakes in the ground that it can attach to and follow. Peter planted stakes of truth in our path so that we could follow and grow straight:

Prepare your mind for action.

Be self-controlled.

Set your hope fully on grace.

Don't conform to evil desires.

Be holy in all you do.

If you desire to grow and become more like Christ, this section of 1 Peter will awaken your heart and encourage you to pursue true growth.

PREPARATION ✝ FOCUS YOUR THOUGHTS

Share a growing story with a friend. It may be gardening, growing up, or growing spiritually during a trying time. Why can growing be such a difficult process? How has your own growth process challenged you?

READING ✝ HEAR THE WORD

As you read this text and prayerfully ask God to reveal His truth to you, you can almost sense Peter turning up the heat. The word *therefore* in verse 13 indicates that the first 12 verses were a setup to his theology (beliefs about God and the things of God), and now he is going to make it clear how we are to live.

If you are underlining key words in your Bible, underline all of the action words like *prepare, set*, and *call*. Remember Peter's audience and the extreme pressure they were under to conform (v. 14). Many of his readers would have been Paul's converts. Others may have been at Pentecost and heard Peter's great sermon.

Find a place where you can read this text aloud. If you are in a group, take turns reading the text one verse at a time.

MEDITATION ☩ ENGAGE THE WORD

Meditate on 1 Peter 1:13-16

Peter said he was writing to "God's elect," so we know they have had a heart experience with Jesus Christ. The next obvious step in their war against sin was the battle of the mind. Like Paul, Peter knew that the victorious Christian would be someone who was "transformed by the renewing of their mind" (Rom. 12:2). If we look at verse 16 as the goal of Christian living, "Be holy, because I am holy," then the commands of verses 13-15 are how we reach that goal. Look at each of these phrases carefully, and think of how they apply to your life today:

Prepare your minds for action. What do you think it means to prepare your mind? Did you face anything in the past two or three days that you were not prepared for spiritually? How did you conquer that battle?

Be self-controlled. We often use the words *exercise self control*. Can you see how self-control gets stronger as we exercise it? Are there areas in your life that are weak and need to be strengthened?

Set your hope fully on the grace to be given to you when Jesus Christ is revealed. Like a compass aimed at true north, we are to remain focused on God's grace. What does this mean to you in your current life situation? How deep is your focus on God's grace?

Do not conform to the evil desires. The Greek word Peter used for *conform* means changeable or unstable. If our foundation is holy, how do we take root in Him and not gravitate toward our old way of living?

Read the excerpt from Leviticus 11, and then read Leviticus 11:41-47. Peter had a great knowledge of Old Testament texts and made a modern-day application for his readers. What do you think it means to "distinguish between the clean and the unclean"? How should the message of Leviticus be applied today?

> I am the Lord who brought you up out of Egypt to be your God; therefore be holy, because I am holy. These are the regulations concerning animals, birds, every living thing that moves in the water and every creature

that moves about on the ground. You must distinguish between the unclean and the clean, between living creatures that may be eaten and those that may not be eaten. —*Leviticus 11:45-47*

Meditate on 1 Peter 1:17-21

What would it cost to redeem the sins of humanity once and for all? What could God possibly give that would be valuable enough to atone for our empty way of life? The words of a famous hymn come to mind, "Nothing but the Blood of Jesus." Peter is reminding us of the infinite value of grace. So what shall we do, as Paul asked in Romans 6:1: "Shall we go on sinning that grace may increase?"

Read the quote from Martin Luther. Where is your sin? How does the message of the quote make you want to change your habits and practices? How does it make you want to pursue holiness?

Either sin is with you, lying on your shoulders, or it is lying on Christ, the Lamb of God. Now if it is lying on your back, you are lost; but if it is resting on Christ, you are free, and you will be saved. Now choose what you want. —*Martin Luther*

Take a closer look at the phrase *reverent fear* in verse 17. Scripture often cautions us to have a healthy fear of God's holiness. Do you have a reverent fear of God? How do you demonstrate this reverent fear in your relationship with Christ? In general, do you think that Christians have lost some of their reverent fear for holy things?

Meditate on 1 Peter 1:22—2:3

Peter is a great encourager. Most of us have at least one person in our lives who always knows what to say to encourage us to keep going. Think about those people. What types of characteristics do these people hold? In these verses Peter uses words from Isaiah 40 (1:24-25) and from David's Psalm 34 (2:3) to comfort and to inspire us. Study these verses slowly and carefully. Notice how Peter incorporates loving others and ridding ourselves of all deceit with holy living.

Read the quote from Lou Barbieri. How was salvation your first taste of God? How have you been feeding and growing on the Word since that first moment?

> Peter is not questioning the salvation of his readers, but he is pointing out that their salvation experience is only the first "taste." The more believers feed on the Word, the more they will learn of its Author.
>
> —Lou Barbieri

Before you leave this text, focus in on the word *crave* in 2:2. Are there times when you crave more of God?

PRAYER ☩ ASK AND LISTEN

Seek the face of God. Ask, "Lord, what are You saying to us today?"

Peter has given us words of wisdom and encouragement that should stir in us a deep desire to be growing spiritually. Spend a few silent minutes allowing God to show you anything in your life that needs to change. Pray for God's power to be fresh and real to you today, so you may follow His will of growth for your life.

CONTEMPLATION ☩ REFLECT AND YIELD

Spiritual growth is not going to just happen. We have to want it and pursue it. Draw a line between where you are spiritually and where you would like to be one month, six months, and a year from now. What will it take to get you there?

GROUP STUDY

- What are you staking your spiritual growth on?

- How are you being formed into the likeness of Christ?

- Think about the areas of your life that could potentially cause your growth to be weakened. How can you release those areas to God?

- If you lived every minute with a reverent fear of the Lord, would you experience spiritual growth? Why, or why not? How would it help your relationship with the Lord?

- If your mind were prepared for action each day, would you win more battles? Why, or why not?

- If God wants to take you to new depths, are you ready to follow Him? Would there be anything holding you back?

- This week, think of one way you can grow in your relationship with God.

SUFFERING AND SUBMITTING: STEPS WORTH FOLLOWING

LISTENING FOR GOD THROUGH 1 PETER 2:11-25

Summary

Submission is often misunderstood in today's culture. Most of the time, the word *submission* brings thoughts of weakness and cowardice into our minds. The word *suffering* ignites similar negative thoughts. We assume those who suffer are doing so because of something they've done wrong.

Notice how Peter challenges popular opinion in the area of suffering and in the area of submission. He shows how submission can be good and how suffering can be experienced by those who are right where God wants them to be. He shows how both of these negatives can turn to positives in God's kingdom.

Earlier in his life, following his newfound Master, Peter would have preferred a good fight to "turning the other cheek." In this text, we see a spiritually mature Peter who has learned the value of fighting with love. His formula for faith sharing—an obedient reflection of the attitude of Jesus—is still the best way to introduce others to Christ.

As you hear and obey the leading of the Holy Spirit through these verses, allow yourself to be reminded that others are watching your attitude and actions.

PREPARATION ✝ FOCUS YOUR THOUGHTS

Take a few minutes to discuss examples of suffering and submission in our culture. Do you think we suffer enough for our faith? Why, or why not?

Do you think we fully understand submission? Why, or why not?

READING ✝ HEAR THE WORD

At a time in history when Roman authority surrounded Christians, Peter's words of submission and suffering carried great weight. The ancient society of Asia Minor, which is now the country known as Turkey, was very status conscious. Power was clearly associated with position.

Even though we are centuries apart, the challenge to practice holiness is still important: Don't sin, live clean lives, be good citizens, respect your elders, and follow the steps of Christ.

As you listen to the Holy Spirit through this text, think of your response to your school, your work, and anyone who is in a position of authority over you. Remember the extreme persecution and extra-mile mind-set demonstrated by Peter in this text.

Notice, however, that Peter is not suggesting that we give in and give up everything we believe in. When he was brought before the Sanhedrin in Acts 4:19 and was commanded not to preach, he replied, "Judge for yourselves whether it is right in God's sight to obey you rather than God."

Always pointing to the Cross and the perfect life of Christ, Peter reminds us to be like Christ who submitted himself even to death for our sins. Following His steps means living a life of love that is the evidence of grace to a lost world.

Read 1 Peter 2:11-25 prayerfully, keeping these issues in mind as you read.

MEDITATION ✝ ENGAGE THE WORD

Meditate on 1 Peter 2:11-17

Have you ever felt that you were in the wrong place at the wrong time? There are some places and situations that can make us feel very awkward and out of place. This is what Peter is trying to describe to a group of struggling first-century Christians. Sin is a foreign land, and heaven is our home.

A simple definition of holiness is to be set apart. In other words, when we live good lives, others will see the contrast, the difference, between the world and those who are followers of Christ.

Notice in verse 12 that there will be people in heaven someday as a result of the way we live. The world is watching us, and they are looking to see the positive impact Christ is having in our lives. How can you use this reminder as a serious call to live the right way?

Read the quote by C. S. Lewis. Have you ever had anyone ask if you were a Christian because they noticed something different about you? Have you ever been around someone who you thought must be a Christian because of the difference you could see in him or her? Explain what made this person different.

> How little people know when they think that holiness is dull. When one meets the real thing, it is irresistible.
>
> —C. S. Lewis

Most of us ask at some point, "What is God's will for my life?" Peter offers a few suggestions in verses 13-17. It is God's will that we submit to every authority. This includes authority in our homes, our churches, our cities, and our countries. It is God's will that we act respectfully toward others. Showing respect to other people shows respect to God. How can this type of living silence those who are opposed to our faith?

Read the quote by Rick Warren. Can you see how submission and respect lead to developing your character and holiness? Think about ways a person can show Christ-honoring respect to his or her leaders.

> *God is more interested in your character than your comfort, and He's more concerned about your holiness than your happiness. So, the question is not, if you'll go through dark times in life; rather it's when you'll go through them.*
>
> —Rick Warren

Meditate on 1 Peter 2:18-20

Submission is a choice we make. We know enough about Peter to know that submission did not come naturally to him.

The word *submission* is seldom used in today's vocabulary. Why do you think that is? Jesus Christ was the greatest example of submission. Think of some examples of Christ's submission. What can we learn from them?

Are there areas of your life where you are resisting the choice of submission? What changes can you make to use your submissive spirit as a witness to unsaved people?

Meditate on 1 Peter 2:21-25

The Christian life is challenging because it constantly goes against the grain of the world. Following the footsteps of Christ (v. 21) may include steps of suffering. Have you ever thought of suffering and servanthood as privileges? When you think of holiness and being more like Christ, can you picture yourself rejoicing while you suffer?

Read the quote by McCheyne. Reflect on times in your life when God used your pain or suffering to minister to others. How has suffering changed your relationship with Christ?

> There is a great want about all Christians who have not suffered. Some flowers must be broken or bruised before they emit any fragrance.
> —Robert Murrey McCheyne

Read Isaiah 53 and take notice of how Peter echoed Isaiah in his writing. As you read, allow God to teach you more about Christ's suffering and how it can change your life.

PRAYER ⚜ ASK AND LISTEN

Seek the face of God. Ask, "Lord, what are You saying to us today?"

When we submit or when we suffer, we are following the footsteps of Christ. As you pray and listen to God, invite the Holy Spirit to show you how your response to difficulty can minister to others.

CONTEMPLATION ⚜ REFLECT AND YIELD

Jesus told us that we are blessed if we suffer (Matt. 5). What difference would it make in your life if you approached all trials as opportunities to be blessed?

Are you spiritually prepared to submit or to suffer with a Christlike attitude?

GROUP STUDY

- What is your own definition of submission? What about suffering?

- Are there ways that you feel like your attitude should be adjusted to reflect the attitude of Christ? How so?

- Is the way you act at school the same way you act at church? Do people at school notice something different about you because you are a Christian?

- Do you trust God's will even when it is painful?

- Discuss times where you have suffered, and how you were blessed by those trials.

- Discuss a time when you submitted to God's will. How did it affect your relationship with Him? How did it affect your relationship with others?

- List three or four people who you know are watching your Christian walk. Write at least one way you can better show them the difference Christ makes in your life.

ROOM FOR ONE
NUMBER ONE
LISTENING FOR GOD THROUGH 1 PETER 3:8-22

Summary

We all have priorities. Balancing school, friends and church can prove to be a challenge, and with these things come a lot of choices and responsibilities.

Peter was aware of how making the right decisions and setting the right priorities can affect our walk with Christ. In difficult and urgent situations he had experienced both the grief of poor decisions and the blessing of choosing correctly.

The process of making Christ-centered choices begins long before the point of decision. Good decision making at critical times is always the result of an earlier commitment to make Christ first in your life (v. 15).

You will have many decisions to make each day. Some are small; many are important. The choices you make reflect your priorities. Looking at your priorities, can you say that Christ is first and foremost in your life?

PREPARATION ⚜ FOCUS YOUR THOUGHTS

Think back on the past several days. What kind of decisions have you made? What do those decisions say about your life? How do they align with the priorities of your heart?

READING ⚜ HEAR THE WORD

Clear instructions for practical holy living may be the best way to describe Peter's message in this text. Like a coach recapping the game plan, he illustrated the steps that will lead to victory.

Peter discussed one of the most common challenges for believers of his era: to live in harmony in a world that despised them. Out of his experience, he gave readers five suggestions for holy living that would attack the world with love: be sympathetic, love as brothers, be compassionate, be humble, and do not repay evil with evil, but with blessing.

These verses are lined with planned repetition. We are reminded of our calling. We are encouraged to endure suffering, because we will be blessed. Most importantly, Peter keeps before us the reason for it all: Christ died for our sins.

The key to surviving in any type of suffering or persecution is setting apart Christ in our hearts. Christ in us, changing us, ruling us, is our best defense against all opposition and temptation.

Read 1 Peter 3:8-22, pause after every verse, and think about its message.

MEDITATION ⚜ ENGAGE THE WORD

Meditate on 1 Peter 3:8-12

Living in biblical community, even in the face of persecution, has always been a Christian's best defense. Peter knew that if we lived right, others would see a difference and want to know more about our relationship with Christ. Have you ever had someone notice that you were a Christian because of the way you were living?

Take a moment to read Psalm 34, especially verses 12-16. Why do you think Peter chose this quote of David?

There is an old song we sing with children that says, "Be careful little eyes what you see." Note the keywords—*see, tongue, speech, eyes, ears,* and *face*—of verses 10-12. How are these words important to us as we demonstrate our faith to others? Are there things you are hearing, seeing, or saying that might hurt your testimony?

Meditate on 1 Peter 3:13-17

Read the quote by Glenn Penner on page 40. Now, as you think about Peter's repeated use of the word *suffer,* how does this change your view of 1 Peter?

The Bible (especially the New Testament) was written by persecuted believers to persecuted believers. This context cannot be ignored without it having profoundly negative implications for how we read and apply the Bible and how we follow Christ individually and corporately. A cross-centered gospel requires cross-carrying messengers. —Glenn Penner

Have you ever suffered as a result of your faith? Do you think that is a good thing? Explain.

Verse 14 addresses an age-old question: Why do good people suffer? Notice the answer in the verses that follow. God uses our suffering, our situations, and how we respond to them to lead others to Christ.

Read the quote from Martin Luther King Jr. How does Dr. King's perspective align with what Peter is telling believers in this passage?

The ultimate measure of a man is not where he stands in moments of comfort and convenience, but where he stands at times of challenge and controversy. —Martin Luther King Jr.

Peter had learned that the only way to spiritual victory was for Christ to be first in his life (v. 15). What are the things that hold a place in your heart? Is there anything that competes with Christ to be first in your life?

Meditate on 1 Peter 3:18-22

When we think of all that Christ has done for us, when we remember the Cross, His suffering, and the power of His resurrection, we find the courage to stand firm through suffering and to expect God to raise us to victory. As you study verse 18, make it personal. Read it this way, "For Christ died for [your name] sins once for all, the righteous for the unrighteous, to bring [your name] to God." How does this change the way you think about this text?

Now, read it again and enter the name of someone you know who is not yet a Christian. Why do you think Peter used the words *all*, and *righteous* and *unrighteous?*

Christ's death and resurrection, the rainbow after the flood, and the symbol of baptism are all illustrations of grace. What is your definition of the word *grace?* How would you illustrate what grace has meant to you? If one of your friends didn't know the word *grace*, how would you explain it to them?

Water is used symbolically in Scripture for salvation, cleansing, and the washing away of sins. Why do you think Peter chose water as an illustration? What other words or terms do we use to describe forgiveness and salvation?

Read the quote by Juan Carlos Ortiz. Can people see the evidence of grace in your life? How does it make you feel to know that others are watching when you are weak?

> In Christ, we live on the trapeze. The whole world should be able to watch and say, "Look how they live, how they love one another. Look how well the husbands treat their wives. And aren't they the best workers in the factories and offices, the best neighbors, the best students?"
>
> —Juan Carlos Ortiz

PRAYER ☦ ASK AND LISTEN

Seek the face of God. Ask, "Lord, what are You saying to us today?"

Setting apart Christ as the first love of your heart is critical to your spiritual formation.

As you pray, write a short letter to Christ that you can keep in your Bible. Simply put into words your desire for Him to always hold the highest place in your life.

CONTEMPLATION  REFLECT AND YIELD

Reflect on your spiritual journey so far. Have there been times in your life when Jesus did not have priority? What have you learned from those experiences? Invite God to take inventory of all that's important to you. Listen closely as the Holy Spirit reveals to you anything you have allowed to come before Christ.

GROUP STUDY

- Are you careful of what you see, touch, and hear?

- What decisions have you made recently that reflect your priorities?

- Are your priorities in the right order? If not, how could you rearrange them?

- What things in your life compete with your relationship with Christ as first position on your list of priorities?

- Have you ever faced persecution for believing what you do?

- Has anyone ever made fun of you for the way you live your life, and the priorities that you keep?

- Take a small piece of paper or a sticky note. Write the words, "Christ must be first in my life." Place this note somewhere you can look at it throughout the week as a reminder of Christ's priority in your life.

Summary

There are many things a Christian *can* do. There are some things a Christian *should* do. But there is one thing that a Christian *must* do: love.

Peter was an intense and passionate disciple of Christ. He had many opportunities to hear Jesus teach about love. He witnessed the Master demonstrating love for the crowds, the outcasts, the religious opposition, the rich, and the poor. Peter wrestled with his own nature of revenge and retaliation, eventually surrendering it to the Spirit. The new Peter now calls us to love above all.

There is no substitute for love. When we suffer, even for doing good things, let us love. When the world hates us for not joining their sin, let us love. When we use our gifts to serve others, let us love. In obedience, listening to God's calling for our lives, let us love.

As you read this passage, meditate on the truth that changed Peter's life: love covers all.

PREPARATION ✝ FOCUS YOUR THOUGHTS

We love God through our worship and obedience. We love ourselves by respecting who God has made us to be. How do we show our love for others?

READING ✝ HEAR THE WORD

Because the Christians during Peter's era didn't follow the lifestyle practices common in that time, followers of Christ were viewed as a threat to society. As a result, Peter told the Christians in Asia Minor to arm themselves with love and the attitude of Christ. It was good advice then, and it is good advice now.

Even though our culture is drastically different than it was during the time of Peter, Christianity is still an ongoing spiritual warfare with seen and unseen enemies. In this text Peter took on the role of general, discussing our best defense and plan of attack. He had learned the way of Christ perfectly. Drawing on lessons learned on the frontlines with Christ, he gave us this plan: arm yourselves with love, because love conquers all.

Throughout chapter 4, Peter's message shows us how passionate and convicted he felt about God's calling. As you read this passage, you will see the following essentials:

Remember Christ's suffering for us.

Honor the Lord with obedient living.

Live to do the will of God.

Serve one another in love.

Rejoice and endure suffering because of Christ.

Read 1 Peter 4:1-19, and consider whether these essentials are important for us to remember today.

MEDITATION ✛ ENGAGE THE WORD

Meditate on 1 Peter 4:1-6

Peter's desire was that we understand the relationship between Christ's sacrifice and our sanctification. The key word in this passage is *since*. Since Christ has won the victory of the Cross, we can arm ourselves with the same battle-winning obedience.

Why do you think Peter chose attitude as something to arm us with? How can our attitude deliver victory or defeat?

Christ died so we might live. Likewise, we must die to sin if we are to live for the will of God. Early Christians understood that the benefit of being a Christian was not success, wealth, or easy living but rather the joy of living a life of service to God. Do you feel as though you are living out God's will for your life? What is your definition of God's will?

Read the quote from Rick Warren. If we are all designed for a purpose, what is God's purpose for your life? How can you stay focused on this purpose?

> The purpose of your life is far greater than your own personal fulfillment, your peace of mind or even happiness. It's far greater than your family, your career, or even your wildest dreams and ambitions. If you want to know why you were placed on this planet, you must begin with God. You were born by his purpose and for his purpose.
> —Rick Warren

Meditate on 1 Peter 4:7-11

Another of Peter's motivations for holy living was the expectation of Christ's return. This sense of urgency should compel the Christian to self-control and prayer for a clean heart. What do you think it means to be clear-minded? How is it related to prayer?

Love covers all. These three words are strategically placed in the heart of Peter's message. After many words of encouragement and warnings to right living, Peter summed it up with the proclamation that love can cover anything. Love is not only at the heart of Peter's message; it is the heart of the gospel, the heart of Christ.

If we love one another with Christ's love, how will we respond to those within Christ's body? How will we respond to those outside the faith? What difference does this kind of love have in real life?

Peter specifically mentioned two gifts necessary for fellowship. First, if we speak, we are to honor God with our words. Second, if we serve, we should serve with determination and with strength from the Lord. Why do you think we are to use our gifts for others? How is using your spiritual gift useful in administering God's grace?

Read the quote by Lou Barbieri. How does this perspective give you a new insight into the kind of service God wants from you? How does it help you put into perspective the contributions of other believers to the Body of Christ?

> We must never forget that ministry takes many forms. Helping people in various ways is ministry! Setting up chairs for a church function is ministry! Stuffing church bulletins on a Friday morning is ministry! All of us can be involved in serving, performing it "by the strength which God supplies." —Lou Barbieri

Meditate on 1 Peter 4:12-19

Suffering is going to come. It came to Jesus, and it will come to His followers. Peter wisely chose to focus on the positive and reminded us of the blessings and rewards of our faith. Why do you think Peter told us not to be surprised at painful trials and suffering? Why should we expect such things?

What reasons do these verses suggest for rejoicing when we share Christ's suffering? Can you think of other reasons?

PRAYER ☦ Ask and Listen

Seek the face of God. Ask, "Lord, what are You saying to us today?"

If Christ is first of all, and if we choose love above all, we will rejoice in any situation. Love is a choice. Bow your heart and ask Christ to speak to you about your love for others.

CONTEMPLATION ☦ Reflect and Yield

Read the quote from Samuel Chadwick on page 51. Do you have that kind of soul, ablaze for God? Does your service follow your passion? How do people see the love of Christ in your life?

Spirit filled souls are ablaze for God. They love with a love that glows. They serve with a faith that kindles. They serve with a devotion that consumes. They hate sin with a fierceness that burns. They rejoice with a joy that radiates. Love is perfected in the fire of God.
—Samuel Chadwick

If Christ changed you today and filled you with the power of His love, what difference would that make in your world? Are you ready for that kind of change?

GROUP STUDY

- Do you find it hard to love certain people? Why? What makes them so difficult to love?

- If there is someone who is difficult to love, how do you overcome that and love them anyway?

- How can you keep an attitude of love at all times, even during the most frustrating situations?

- What are ways you minister to others? What can you do this week to extend your ministry to reach more people?

- How would the dynamic of your youth group change if everyone acted as if love covers all?

- How would the dynamic of your youth group change if everyone served determinedly with a heart full of love and compassion?

- Think of one loving act you can do this week. Then pray, asking God to give you the strength to carry out that loving act.

LIFTED BY HUMILITY
LISTENING FOR GOD THROUGH 1 PETER 5:1-14

Summary

If experience is the best teacher, then Peter had been taught well. How many times had he taken matters into his own hands? How often did his impulsive nature get the best of him? Now, an older, wiser apostle, Peter gives a strong message of instruction, and encouragement.

The urgency in Peter's words reflected the extreme opposition his readers were facing. It was extremely difficult to belong to a house church in Pontus, Galatia, Cappadocia, Asia, and Bithynia, and required a great deal of courage and faith. Peter reminded the church of Christ's suffering, a believer's proper humility, and daily holy living.

In this climate of Christian persecution, Peter knew the importance of solid leadership. In times of difficulty leaders must lead. Leading like Christ involves humility, serving, and the heart of a shepherd.

Extreme days require extreme faith. Trials will come. They may be political, social, or spiritual. They might affect our safety, our health, or our relationships. The question is not *if* but *when* and *how* will we handle them?

PREPARATION ☩ Focus Your Thoughts

What does humility look like? Think of one person in our culture who represents humility and discuss what makes that person humble.

READING ☩ Hear the Word

Take a close look at the wording of this text. It's easy to see that Peter listened intently to Jesus' teachings. Terms like *shepherd*, *flock*, and *humility* all echo God's plan for effective leadership.

In times of crisis the flock will always look to the shepherd. Leaders' reactions to difficult situations will either encourage or discourage their followers. New Testament elders were respected for their spiritual maturity. The evidence of this maturity would have been seen in the display of humility and grace during high-pressure situations.

The word *shepherd* in this passage carries the same meaning as Jesus' use of the term in John 10. It represents both the relationship of elders to their people and of God to His people.

Jesus illustrated how the Good Shepherd will lay down His life when the wolf attacks the flock. With parallel thoughts, Peter's words caution us to be alert to the prowling enemy. Caution when meeting resistance will protect the flock and the shepherd.

Read 1 Peter 5:1-14.

MEDITATION ⚜ ENGAGE THE WORD

Meditate on 1 Peter 5:1-4

Peter addressed the elders—those in leadership—with encouragement to care for and serve others. When you think of Christian leadership, what words come to mind? Why do you think Peter calls for care and service from the elders? What could Christian leaders do today to show more humility and concern for others?

Read the quote by Albert Pike. How did Peter serve others? How have the results of Peter's work lived on despite his death in the first century? What are you concerned with beyond your own needs that will make a difference for eternity?

> *What we have done for ourselves alone dies with us; what we have done for others and the world remains forever.* —Albert Pike

With a word of hope, Peter reminds us that Christ will one day return, and we will receive the crown of glory. Jesus wore a crown of thorns with humility. What do you think the crown of glory will be? How does the hope of eternal reward affect the way we live today?

Meditate on 1 Peter 5:5-9

Submission, respect, humility, and grace are all necessary for healthy relationships, especially relationships within the Body of Christ. Considering the pressure these believers were facing, a strong fellowship and love for one another was their only hope for success.

Note especially Peter's instruction to, "clothe yourselves with humility." How do you wear humility? What other lessons can you draw from this phrase? How can we be more intentional about wearing humility?

Read the quote by Andrew Murray. Can you recall a time when you felt a perfect quietness in your heart? What is the relationship between our heart and humility? How would it affect your troubles or disappointments if you were to "humble yourself in the sight of the Lord" (v. 6)?

> *Humility is perfect quietness of heart. It is for me to have no trouble; never to be fretted or vexed or irritated or sore or disappointed.* —Andrew Murray

If we would remember God's strength and all the times He has covered us with His hand, we would be quicker to cast all of our anxieties on Him. God cares enough for us to save us. He cares enough for us to protect us. He cares enough for us to invite us to live free from the weight of sin and the devil's attacks. Our part in this divine protection is that we must exercise self-control. How can we do this? How can we anticipate the evil one and then resist his schemes?

Explain in a sentence or two what it means to be spiritually alert. How is burden-free living related to resisting the devil?

Take an inventory of any cares, worries, or burdens that you have not turned over to Christ. What are some ways that you can practice care-casting?

Meditate on 1 Peter 5:10-14

Sometimes what people need to hear the most is a word of hope. The suffering Peter's churches were enduring was very real, but, in terms of eternity, would only last a little while. Every believer in every age has the hope of eternal glory in Jesus Christ. How does an eternal perspective give you hope in whatever troubles you most today?

In verse 10 we are reminded of God's calling on our lives. This, too, is a recurring theme of great importance throughout Peter's writing. Peter was acknowledging that the Christian journey will be difficult. Ridicule, persecution, suffering, temptation, and discouragement are normal and to be expected. Yet, he pleaded with his readers to return to their calling. Why are our individual callings so important?

Read the Oswald Chambers quote. According to Chambers, what are Christians called to do? What have you been called to do in your own life? How does this change of perspective benefit you? What can you do to keep your calling clear and fresh in your heart?

> *God's call is for you to be His loyal friend, for whatever purpose He has for your life.* —Oswald Chambers

PRAYER ☦ Ask and Listen

Seek the face of God. Ask, "Lord, what are You saying to us today?"

Our tendency is to try harder and do more. God is calling us to trust more and depend on Him. Silently pray and commit to a new level of humility and trust in Christ.

CONTEMPLATION ☦ Reflect and Yield

What areas of your life would be most affected by a renewed passion for Christlike humility? Have you fully surrendered all areas of your life to the lordship of Christ?

GROUP STUDY

- What can you say about your own character and humility?

- How does this culture make it so hard to be humble?

- Are there areas of your life you have not allowed God to take control of?

- What are ways you can let go of these areas and give God permission to take control?

- As a group, discuss the most meaningful part of the chapter for each person. Why were each of those things meaningful, and how will you use those parts to improve your walk with Christ?

- Imagine if each member of your youth group released all anxieties humbly to God. How would this change the atmosphere of the group?

- Write down three ways you can express a humble attitude in your daily life this week.

THE GREAT ESCAPE
LISTENING FOR GOD THROUGH 2 PETER 1:1-21

Summary

Freedom is a precious and valuable thing. Once you've experienced freedom, nothing could ever take its place. The freedom Peter celebrated with his churches is the greatest freedom of all—freedom from sin.

Sin's escape route is paved by the righteousness of Christ. Peter now fully realized that it's about Christ and the power of His cross, not about what we have done. Focus on the Cross, and you can flee from sin.

Like someone being called to give witness in court, Peter testified of his firsthand experience with Jesus. His message: Meet the Messiah and you will want to make every effort to live a life of obedience and worship. Like Peter, you know that the snares, traps, and vices of this world are everywhere. Follow God's path for your life and you will discover victorious, holy living.

PREPARATION ⚱ Focus Your Thoughts

Have you ever had to escape from any type of danger or close call? How did you feel? What did it teach you? Applying that lesson to your spiritual life, what spiritual precautions can you apply to avoid danger?

READING ⚱ Hear the Word

Reminding was a common approach in ancient teaching styles. In this text you will see recurring themes: godliness, calling, self-control, eternity, and Christ's return. Peter used this letter to remind his contemporaries—and us—of many truths we've already learned.

In this second book, rather than focusing on suffering, Peter turns our attention to the amazing salvation Christ offers. Peter reminds his readers that the reason for pressing on remains the same: Christ has accomplished His work in us and for us.

There is an important relationship to note between Peter's use of the word *knowledge* and his list of virtues in verses 5-7. As we grow in knowledge and progressively add these Christlike traits to our lives, we will be able to escape any evil.

Read 2 Peter 1:1-21.

MEDITATION ☦ ENGAGE THE WORD

Meditate on 2 Peter 1:1-21

Although Peter was an apostle and elder, he identified himself as a servant. His grasp of the gospel is evident—the last shall be first. What things come to mind when you think of the word *servant?* Why do you think Peter began his letter this way?

The knowledge of God and Christ is an important theme in this writing. This is important theology for all believers to understand. As we learn more about Christ and mature in wisdom, we will be able to grow in grace and peace. That's why Peter tells us to be eager. Godliness is not automatic. It requires desire, discipline, and determination to be more like the Master every day.

Read the quote from Leonard Ravenhill. Are you hungry for biblical knowledge? How are you filling this hunger? Are you hungry for God? Do you agree with Ravenhill's opinion of how this hunger needs to be filled?

> *A man may study because his brain is hungry for knowledge, even Bible knowledge. But he prays because his soul is hungry for God.* —Leonard Ravenhill

How would you describe spiritual knowledge? How do we increase our knowledge of God? What are some practical ways for believers to apply knowledge?

Earlier, Peter had referred to the devil as a roaring lion. In verses 5, 6, and 7 he gives us an escape route from all snares and temptations. It's not enough to simply read these verses or to even memorize them. Peter forcefully encourages us to go after these qualities with everything we have. If we don't, we are an easy prey for the enemy.

Examine each quality from verses 5, 6, and 7. Compare these verses to Galatians 5:22. Do you think there is significance in the order that Peter listed these virtues?

Meditate on 2 Peter 1:12-21

Some things will last forever, and some things won't. As Peter reflected on his own mortality, he reminds readers of something that will never change and never die—the Word of God. It was critical to the Early Church to defend God's Word as holy and unchangeable. Heretics and doubters would challenge it often. Even after Peter's death, the Truth would remain alive and well for centuries to come.

What does it mean to you that God's Word has survived all challenges from that day to now? Why does it matter that His Word remains the one constant in this world?

In verse 12 Peter challenges believers to be, "firmly established in the truth." What do you think he meant? How do we become established as believers? How can we show that we're established?

Read the quote by A. W. Tozer. Do you agree with it? Do you think this is practical for all Christians? Do you think most believers have a good understanding of the entire Bible? How much of the Bible do you know and put into practice daily?

> The Word of God well understood and religiously obeyed is the shortest route to spiritual perfection. And we must not select a few favorite passages to the exclusion of others. Nothing less than a whole Bible can make a whole Christian.   —A. W. Tozer

A firsthand, eyewitness account is always the most powerful testimony. Peter's words are filled with energy as he recounts being there with Christ. To Peter, knowledge of Christ wasn't just based on written word but also by having a relationship with the risen Lord.

Note the key elements of Peter's personal testimony: He was an eyewitness to the Crucifixion (v. 16). He heard the Father speak from heaven (v. 17). He validated those experiences by confirming it through the word of the prophets from the Old Testament (v. 19).

How important was Peter's testimony to his churches and to the Early Church? How important has this testimony been in holding up scriptural truth across the centuries?

What are three key elements to your testimony? Can you concisely and expressively describe your knowledge of Christ to another?

Read the quote from Stuart Briscoe. What do you think Briscoe means by *audible evidence?* What do you think he means by *visible evidence?*

> A witness is someone who by explanation and demonstration gives audible and visible evidence of what he has seen and heard without being deterred by the consequences of his action.   —Stuart Briscoe

Who are some great witnesses from Scripture? Who are some modern-day witnesses of Christianity? What makes their testimony real and evident to all?

PRAYER ☦ ASK AND LISTEN

Seek the face of God. Ask, "Lord, what are You saying to us today?"

Peter set an example of one who had escaped the traps of sin and was growing in the knowledge of Christ. In silent prayer, ask God to protect you and free you from the enemy.

CONTEMPLATION 🕆 REFLECT AND YIELD

If you lived with less sin and more of Christ, how would this transform your life and relationships? Are you committed to pursuing more of Christ on a daily basis?

GROUP STUDY

- How would you rate your knowledge of the Bible?

- How does your knowledge of the Bible affect your relationship with Christ?

- What are the characteristics of a modern-day witness of Christianity?

- What are some of the obstacles to our growth in the knowledge of Christ?

- What are the ways we can overcome those obstacles and grow in our knowledge of Christ?

- What is an example of the "roaring lion ready to devour"? How can we avoid being devoured?

- Discuss one thing you will do this week to keep your eyes on Christ and avoid falling into the trap of sin?

CLEANING DAY
LISTENING FOR GOD THROUGH 2 PETER 3:1-18

SUMMARY

"I'll be back" is a common catch phrase in our culture. It's also a powerful theme from the mouth of the Savior. The hope of the return of Christ was Peter's fuel for daily living.

Good leaders know their people, and they know what their people need to hear at just the right time. Peter offered encouragement to Christians who were losing their jobs, their land, and those who were being falsely accused, threatened and imprisoned on behalf of their faith. He told them to look beyond their present reality and keep their eyes focused on eternity with Christ.

Peter knew the value of continued personal and spiritual growth. He wasn't just watching the sky for Christ's return. He was making every effort to live toward holiness, and to urge others toward that same goal.

There were many defining moments in Peter's disciple years. Listening to him in this text, we can hear how he was impacted by the ascension of Jesus. Knowing Christ had gone ahead to heaven didn't discourage Peter. It only drove him to live with greater intensity.

Though life is hard, there will be great reward someday in heaven. Remain faithful. Be on your guard. Live right. Because Christ has gone on before, He will soon return to take His own to be with Him forever in an amazing eternity.

PREPARATION ☦ Focus Your Thoughts

Usually, when we are expecting company, there are things we do in preparation. If Jesus were coming to your place tonight, what would you do to get ready?

READING ☦ Hear the Word

Some of the false teachings of Peter's time played down the concept of a future judgment. If Christ wasn't coming back any time soon, there would be more time for immoral living. Peter challenged this thinking straight on because he knew how easy it can be to drift morally from where we ought to be.

Peter, not known for his patience, reminds us of the reason for God's patience: salvation. By quoting Psalm 90:4, Peter reminds us of our need to be patient with the Lord as we live expecting His return.

Typical of other New Testament writing, Peter's thoughts on the future are always accompanied by thoughts of daily holy living.

Read 2 Peter 3:1-18, taking brief notes as you read the text. Pause after each verse, and record one or two things Christians ought to do to be ready for Christ's return. If you are participating in a group, compare your notes and discuss.

MEDITATION ⚜ ENGAGE THE WORD

Meditate on 2 Peter 3:1-7

Peter was wrapping up his writing, his ministry, and his life. He knew the end was near, and wanted his readers to know that although he was soon to die, the Word and the truth of Jesus Christ would remain and maintain them during difficult days.

So there would be no guessing, he clearly stated the purpose of his writing: wholesome thinking. After all, godly thinking leads to godly living. Many times over, God's leaders and God's people have proven that when their heads and hearts are right with the Lord, they can defeat any enemy.

What words would you use to describe wholesome thinking? How does a clear, holy mind-set protect us from evil, suffering, and judgment?

Read the quote from Duncan Campbell. How would a greater commitment to holiness change your relationships? How would it change your community? Your youth group?

> A baptism of holiness, a demonstration of godly living is the crying need of our day.   —Duncan Campbell

In verses 3-7, Peter reminds us of the eternal power of God's Word. Whenever our faith is challenged, we can rest assured that God's Word existed before the earth was formed, and it will remain long after this earth is gone. Peter's convictions were fueled by the impact of Old Testament writing and his passion to see God's Word continue in the hearts and lives of believers everywhere.

Read Genesis 1, and compare it with 2 Peter 3.

Meditate on 2 Peter 3:8-9

God is a patient God. He is patient with us on a daily basis. He is patient with humanity in light of eternity. Jesus had many opportunities to teach Peter the value of patience. Even though Peter lived with the urgency of Christ's return, he also knew that God wants as many as possible to hear the gospel message.

Do a word search on *patience* throughout Scripture. Compare examples of God's patience with examples of our own need to be patient. How is patience a reflection of godliness?

Read John 3:16. Why do you think Peter is emphasizing patience to his churches?

Meditate on 2 Peter 3:10-13

The only thing God is going to rescue from this world is souls. Everything else will eventually be destroyed. This being so, when it's all said and done what matters most is the condition of our hearts before God.

Read the quote by Dietrich Bonhoeffer. How can dying to ourselves be instrumental in leading others to new life? What is the symbolism between Christ's death and resurrection and our need to die to sin? How would you explain this to a non-Christian?

> When Christ calls a man, he bids him come and die.
> —*Dietrich Bonhoeffer*

Peter used a word picture of a thief in the night to describe the return of Christ. This is similar to Christ's own picture in Matthew 24:43-44. What are some suggestions of this imagery? If Christ could return at any moment, how does that affect the way we live?

Read the quote from Vance Havner. How do his words describing eternity show a consistency with Peter's purpose and conclusion in this chapter? How does the perspective of the new heaven and new earth Peter described in verse 13 change everything about how we face trials, suffering, temptation, sin, even death in this life?

> I find the last miles to be the best. When it's twilight on the trail, remember that the other side of the sunset is sunrise. The other side of evening is morning; beyond death is life. One hour in heaven, and we shall be ashamed that we ever grumbled. —Vance Havner

Read Luke 12:39-40. How does the unexpectedness and immediacy of Christ's return make you feel? How does it make you want to live today?

Peter introduced an amazing truth in verse 12. He said we can actually play a role in fast-forwarding the return of Christ. We may not fully understand this verse now, but there are at least three things we know we can be doing: We can pray. We can live holy lives. We can share the gospel with as many people as possible. What are some other things believers can do as we expect the return of Christ?

Meditate on 2 Peter 3:14-18

Notice Peter's use of the word *since*. Whenever we see that word we know Peter is going to support his teaching with encouragement for practical holy living. In this text, what are the key thoughts that follow the word *since*? How are these thoughts consistent with all that he's written in both of the Epistles?

How important are Peter's final words to a young and suffering congregation? How important are they to you?

PRAYER ☦ ASK AND LISTEN

Seek the face of God. Ask, "Lord, what are You saying to us today?"

Peter's parting reminder for all believers is that we would live spotless and blameless lives. Enter God's presence in prayer, and invite the Holy Spirit to do His cleansing, purifying work in your life.

CONTEMPLATION ☦ REFLECT AND YIELD

Are you living as though Christ could return at any moment? Will you surrender all and commit to listening more intently to His voice?

Group Study

- How would you feel if Christ came back today? Would you be ready?

- Is it easy to forget that this is just a temporary home for us? How does it encourage you to know that Christ is coming back for us?

- Would you consider yourself a wholesome thinker? How can you get rid of the things that cloud your thoughts?

- Does the condition of your heart reflect a spotless and blameless life? If not, what things need to happen in order for that to change?

- Since daily holy living requires confession, transparency, and accountability, commit to meet with someone in your group to discuss your spiritual goals.

- How have the words of 1 & 2 Peter had an affect on your relationship with God and others?